What C

by Wiley Blevins

Jason Way Photography/Moment Open/Getty Images

My balloon can pop.

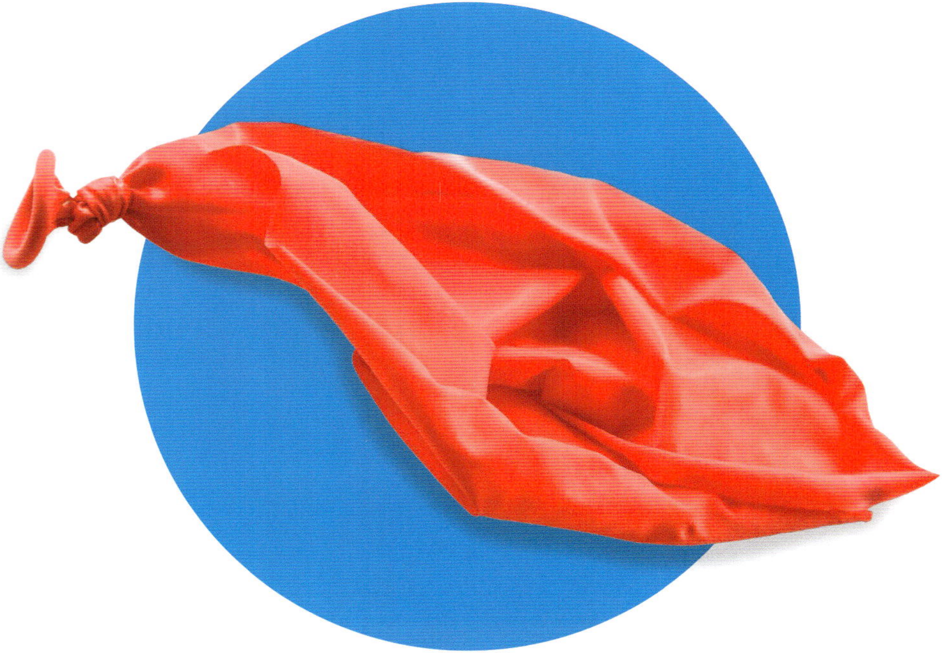

Africa Studio/Shutterstock.com

Pop!

Blend Images/Alamy

My bubble can pop.

Jason Way Photography/Moment Open/Getty Images

Pop!

Tony Cordoza/Alamy

My pot can pop.

Matt Matthews/iStock/Getty Images

Pop! Pop! Pop!